"CANDID QUOTES"

165 Quotes to Live By

_____

By Bobbi Hall

Version 1.0

Dedication

This book is dedicated to those who need to wake up and start living the life they could live!

And, to my Mom who told me weeks before she died, "Bobbi!" "You are destined for greatness!"

As she took notice of my unwavering resilience and unending perseverance to equip myself to be successful in this life.

Table of Contents

Foreword

By Lionnel Yamentou

I first met Bobbi Hall during a workshop I was leading in an organization we are both members of. She was seated in the first row of audience members, and her enthusiastic and friendly presence made a tremendous contribution to the success of the workshop.

Bobbi insisted we take a selfie after that workshop and that was the beginning of a great friendship. I know Bobbi to be a "Daring Dreamer", and this book is one of her many dreams realized.

When Bobbi sent me the final draft of this book on which she had worked for countless hours, only after reading the first few quotes I knew that this was coming from Bobbi's heart.

As much as the thoughts in the next pages will make you laugh, learn and think, allow yourself to meditate and reflect deeply about what they mean to you; that's how you will get the greatest value from this gift from Bobbi.

Preface

"My Candid Quotes" by Bobbi Hall is a compilation of quotes that have taken root in me and are constantly in my head. Some were planted in me by my Father and my Grandmother.

"My Candid Quotes" manifested and landed in this book as a result of a sudden intrusion of simultaneous traumatic events going on in my life, and shocking behaviors I was observing and recipient to.

Enjoy these lessons I have learned and revelations to live by.

I hope you take notes.

My prayer is for you to have your own awakening and reap the benefits.

Enjoy reading, mediating and "living" the life you could live, via, "My Candid Quotes."

Introduction

I am grateful I get to get up every day and make choices. Lately, I've really tried to make it a habit to say, "I'm not in jail, I'm not in the hospital and every day, I get to make choices!"

We make countless decisions each day; from the moment we wake up until we rest our heads on a pillow. We get to create options for ourselves every single day. What a joy, what a blessing, what a privilege.

Ultimately, we are all responsible for our own individual choices. "There is only one person responsible for the quality of our lives and that is you!" (Jack Canfield)

As I write this, I am continuously amazed at the on-going results of my choice to make an investment in learning what it even meant to make good, right, healthy choices. That one choice led me to make another choice; to first, start with what my gut knew was broken in me. That one choice led me to make more choices to equip myself to be successful as a person and in life.

The following quotes have been part of that journey.

Chapter 1
"Bobbi's Quotes"

No. 1

"Channel your hurt and pain, disappointment and anger into fulfilling your dreams and getting what you want."

No. 2

"Don't listen to others' "shoulds" for your life; make a plan and have the courage to pursue what is right for you."

No. 3

"What's happened to you is not
nearly as important as what's
happened "in" you... because
remember... you diligently seek the
wisdom of God."

No. 4

"Times of darkness are a gift; choose
to keep your light turned on; bright
and shining."

No. 5

"Don't waste your breath and energy talking about junk and people you cannot change."

No. 6

"Don't spend time blaming the system; change the system."

No. 7

"Organizations who don't want to "do" or "be" better are a waste of my/your time and will die; don't choose to die with them."

No. 8

"What someone says they feel about you and the way they behave toward you, says everything about them."

No. 9

"Self-centered, self-absorbed, self-serving, self-promoting, ego-centric, me-centered, prideful people; are a waste of my time."

No. 10

"To be defensive is to be immature."

No. 11

"Disrespecting another is the measure of your spiritual immaturity."

No. 12

"When you claim to be a Christian and you are rude to others, you are a hypocrite."

No. 13

"What is in your behavior is in your heart."

No. 14

"To know one's character is to see their behavior."

No. 15

"Deny your weaknesses; determine your denial, direct your destiny."

No. 16

"To not strengthen your weaknesses is to reject God."

No. 17

"Reveal your bad behavior; reveal your character."

No. 18

"To repent is: sorry is as sorry does."

No. 19

"Admitting but not changing, is a lie."

No. 20

"Repent, admit, reflect; bear fruit, change; wear the fruit."

No. 21

"Your future is your past when you do not change."

No. 22

"Internal true desire to change is to not project onto others, your character flaws."

No. 23

"Channel your aggression in acceptable ways and you will prosper."

No. 24

"Proceed with caution... those who resist growth."

"Cowards blame others, for everything; Cowards accuse others of being perfect."

"To not earn one's trust is to be prideful."

No. 27

"Welcoming questions about your trustworthiness is to be truly trustworthy."

No. 28

"Close your ears to feedback; stunt your growth."

No. 29

"Those who are open to an audit of their character are truly serious about growing; those who don't, won't."

No. 30

"If you don't do what you say are going to do this is who you are."

No. 31

"Sooner or later, your character leaks out."

No. 32

"Safe people are stable and reliable and bad company corrupts good character."

No. 33

"Don't ask what you do for a living, ask what do you live to do?"

No. 34

"When you hear someone say, "I have no choice" run the other way; in fact, leave skid marks!"

"Any organization with a blind eye to disrespectful, bullying behavior is blind, deaf, and dumb!"

"Toxic environments and toxic people are the <u>best</u> teachers."

No. 37

"What begins in childhood might become a break down and might end in a break up and result in a breakthrough."

No. 38

"Trust destructs when someone has violated your soul."

No. 39

"The bullies from yesterday are the bullies of today."

No. 40

"The workplace is the same sandbox from childhood, full of the same dysfunctional children; only everybody looks like an adult."

No. 41

"Anyone who is associated with an organization who tacitly allows bullying is an accessory to a crime."

No. 42

"If you don't take care of the inside what comes out on the outside is "Oh Dear----" not going to be good!"

No. 43

"Speak the truth in Love."

No. 44

"Silence… is the sound of creativity… at its best."

No. 45

"People who are consistently inconsistent are not well."

No. 46

"Controllers are out of control."

No. 47

"Looming below the surface is
chronic distraction; which is stress."

No. 48

"Successful people pause..........
deliberately...........in order to remain
successful."

No. 49

"A stable friend is like a stable tree and deflects us from disaster."

No. 50

"Lack of wisdom, lack of insight, lack of education, lack of consciousness and self-awareness, lack of desire to improve yourself and change; makes you a bobble-head!"

No. 51

"Being active is not necessarily productive."

No. 52

"Doing nothing is something."

No. 53

"An organization that puts profits before people is pathetic."

No. 54

"Every road has 2 paths; integrity is what it takes to take the right path."

No. 55

"Integrity is; doing what you say you
are going to do; those who do not,
will fail."

No. 56

"Learn to be content and happy
alone. You have no business being
with someone else until you do.
Learn to be your own best friend and
entertainment and hone in on the
things you love to do and do them! It
is probable you will spend a chunk of
your life alone."

No. 57

"If you hang out with losers, they will teach you a lot; how you will go down with their ship."

No. 58

"If you are a part of something that is dishonest, you are that something."

No. 59

"Healthy safe relationships are not without confrontation."

No. 60

"Your enemies are the yellow brick road to your success."

No. 61

"Successful people are self-aware and are deliberate in changing their bad behavior."

No. 62

"Healing without grief and grief without support means not to heal."

No. 63

"To save one from ultimate
destruction is to confront him/her."

No. 64

"Self-centeredness in relationships
breeds no fruit."

"Garnering wisdom and discernment in character is your work behind finding safe people."

No. 66

"For your happiness, hang out with people who are happy people."

No. 67

"If you keep hearing someone say,
"God this, God that, God, God, God,
Oh but God.…and you see the devil,
they are not well."

No. 68

"When someone keeps calling you
"perfect" you're doing something
very, very right."

"Hanging out with people who are never accountable, self-medicate, surround themselves with "stuff" and do meaningless activities means you need to wake up!"

"Empathy" is a commodity today. No one knows where you have been in your booties, but those "rare" people who listen, try to put themselves in your booties and then call you and check on you knowing you are in pain, are a gem; hang on to them."

No. 71

"If you don't sit up straight and stand up straight you are choosing pre-mature death."

No. 72

"If you don't take time to be still and listen; you are choosing pre-mature death."

"If you don't take time to learn how to be spiritually, physically, financially, emotionally and mentally well, you are choosing <u>serious</u> pre-mature death."

"If you are someone who has to boast all about yourself, fails to keep your commitments, bases your actions on personal gain and lies when you are confronted, I am afraid for you."

"When you meet someone whose three favorite words are: "I", "Me" and "My" ------- run the other way!"

"The best way to encourage and comfort someone is to remind them to: trust their intuition and that what they are going thru will pass and is only temporary and is guaranteed to make them stronger and to not give up! Don't say, "I don't know what to say!" – "I don't know what to say!" – "I don't know what to say!"-----------

No. 77

"Those who listen, seek to understand and take a genuine interest in others and show it, will prosper."

No. 78

"If you are your "job" and sacrifice your mind, body and soul, you are out of balance and an idiot!"

No. 79

"If you are not willing to stand up for what is right; then sit the hell down."

No. 80

"When someone is quick to respond Without seeking to understand and learn the facts and responds saying, "You should..., you need to..., agh, well, ugh, why don't you..., have you ever thought about this... or that......? And they are referring to you, press delete and run!"

No. 81

"Don't ignore negative energy or vibration(s) you sense from someone... especially, when they haven't even opened their mouth!– hello –! RED FLAG!"

No. 82

"You can get a cat or a dog, or some other pet. You can get a husband, a wife, a girlfriend, a boyfriend or a blow-up doll-----
You can spend your time doing meaningless things and surround yourself with lots of meaningless stuff. But if you do not love the core of who you are; what you get is...
N-O-T-H-I-N-G!!!!!!"

No. 83

"There is one thing that is always right and that is my gut. My intuition is the motor of my soul."

No. 84

"Bring on the jealous, the envious and those who covet – They are my motivation to succeed!"

"When you work on yourself, it shows. The less than few people who celebrate you in this life will somehow let you know that it shows, but it is the "jealous" that really show you it shows."

No. 86

"Most don't get a great start. Be determined to have a great finish."

Chapter 2
Family Quotes
"Daddy"

No. 1

"You eat a ton of sh–t a year!"

No. 2

"Sh–t or get off the pot!"

No. 3

"I didn't do it! Not me, I didn't do it!"
(sarcastic)

No. 4

"There is an "A-hole" around every
corner!"

No. 5

"There are no free rides!"

No. 6

"There are no free meal tickets!"

No. 7

"Look in the mirror!"

No. 8

"Don't get pregnant! Learn how to provide for yourself: be self-sufficient, independent and on your own! If you find someone to make your life partner, make sure he has his sh-t (act) together!"

No. 9

"When you're ready to share your life with a partner, make sure he is <u>worthy</u> of you!"

No. 10

"Don't ever, ever, ever and I mean ever!... depend on a man for anything! And... I mean anything!... ever!" "Ever!"

No. 11

"Don't get distracted!"

No. 12

"Make a decision!"

No. 13

"Get an education! Get a college degree! Unless you want to work for minimum wage!"

No. 14

"Don't get into debt!"

No. 15

"If you screw up, you will pay!"

No. 16

"Everybody's an expert!"
(sarcastic)

No. 17

"Put your money where your mouth is!"

No. 18

"Don't wallow!"

Family Quotes
"Granny"
(with a New York accent)

No. 1

"It's always somethin!"

No. 2

"If it's not one thing, it's another!"

No. 3

"I can't be bothered!"

No. 4

"Stop the world, I want to get off!"

Chapter 3
"My Favorite Quotes"

No. 1

"As long as your energy goes to
making something better, it's worth
the sacrifice"
– Mark Anthony, American singer,
actor, record and television producer

No. 2

"When doors are opened wide and
opposition & adversaries walk in,
favor is on the way!"
– Joel Osteen, American preacher and
televangelist. He is the Senior Pastor
of Lakewood Church, the largest
Protestant church in the United
States, in Houston, Texas

No. 3

"Stay in it… to win it!" – Joel Osteen

No. 4

"The bigger the burden the bigger the blessing!"
   – Joel Osteen

No. 5

"Doing... doing... doing... will never heal your being" – unknown

No. 6

"The health of our minds deserves the same attention as the health of our bodies"
– Toni Wilkey (My Yoga Instructor)

No. 7

"It's not how many times you fall down; it's how many times you get back up!" – unknown

No. 8

"Keep the vision, enjoy the process, don't worry about the outcome, and trust your higher power" – Toni Wilkey (My Yoga Instructor)

No. 9

"Uncertainty is certain but
possibilities remain"
– Toni Wilkey (My Yoga Instructor)

No. 10

"Dreams are illustrations from the
book your soul is writing about you"
– Marsha Norman, American
playwright, screenwriter & novelist

"When your desires are strong enough you will possess superhuman powers to achieve"
– Napoleon Hill, American author & impresario

"Victory belongs to the most persevering"
– Napoleon Bonaparte, French military leader

No. 13

"Great things are <u>not</u> done by
impulse, but by a series of small
things brought together."
– Vincent Van Gough, Dutch painter

No. 14

"Your big opportunity may be right
where you are right now"
– Napoleon Hill

No. 15

"Never make excuses. Always wake up with a smile knowing that today you are going to have fun accomplishing what others are too afraid to do"
     – unknown

No. 16

"Excuses are the nails to build your house of failure"
     – unknown

No. 17

"Excuses will always be there;
opportunity will not"
– unknown

No. 18

"If it is important to you, you will find
a way, if not; you will find an excuse"
– unknown

"Make excuses, don't expect to
   excel"
      – unknown

"Hard work beats talent; when talent
fails to work"
– Kevin Durante, American basketball
   player Oklahoma City Thunder

No. 21

"Well done is better than well said"
– Ben Franklin, founding father of the
U.S.

No. 22

"Surfing the waters is much easier
than resisting the waters"
– Toni Wilkey (My Yoga Instructor)

No. 23

"Creating tension takes away needed
    energy"
– Toni Wilkey (My Yoga Instructor)

No. 24

"It's time to be the person you were
    meant to be"
        – unknown

No. 25

"Your actions... are... your priorities"
– Mahatma Gandhi

No. 26

"You try you fail, you try you fail, the greatest failure is when you stop trying"
– unknown

No. 27

"The biggest failure beats the hell out
of never trying"
– unknown

No. 28

"One of the realities in life is that if
you can't trust a person at all points,
you can't truly trust him/her at any
point"
– Cheryl Biehl, author of "I Can't Do
Everything!"

"People who hide their lack of integrity for awhile... are <u>always</u> found out"
– John C. Maxwell, author, speaker, pastor

No. 30

"Character is not created in a crisis, it's found out; everything comes to a head when you're under pressure"---
John C. Maxwell

"Character is made in the small moments of our lives. Anytime you break a moral principle, you create a small crack in the foundation of your integrity"
   – 19th century clergyman Phillips
            Brooks

No. 32

"A man must be measured by the strength of his/her character, not the weight of his credentials"
   – John C. Maxwell

"Two people can grow up in the same environment, even in the same household, and one will have integrity and the other won't. Ultimately, you are responsible for your choices. Your circumstances are as responsible for your character as a mirror is for your looks. What you see reflects who you are"
     – John C. Maxwell

"Positive people have positive happen in their lives, negative people have negative happen in their lives"
– Toni Wilkey (My Yoga Instructor)

"If you change the way you look at things, the things you look at change"
– Wayne Dyer, American philosopher, self help author & motivational, speaker

"There are no drive-thru biggie size breakthroughs; you gotta go through to get through"
   – Joyce Meyer, charismatic bible teacher, author and speaker

"To not choose a path of integrity, is
to choose the road to ruin"
– John C. Maxwell

"To not choose to seek and become
spiritually whole is to be mentally,
emotionally, physically, relationally
and financially unwell"
– Rick Warren, Richard Duane "Rick"
Warren is an American evangelical
Christian pastor and author. He is the
founder and senior pastor of Saddleback
Church, an evangelical mega church in
Lake Forest, California

"Without love, there can be no connection, no future and no success; together"
– John C. Maxwell

"Encouragement is oxygen for the soul"
– John C. Maxwell

"Lack of encouragement hinders a person from living a healthy productive life"
   – John C. Maxwell

No. 42

"Self confidence is the first great requisite to great undertakings"
– Sam Johnson-18th Century writer-critic

"Keep away from people who try to belittle your ambitions"
– Mark Twain, American author and humorist

No. 44

"There are "lawn mowers", People who have good intentions but are self-absorbed... who mow their own lawns but never help others. Then there are "life-enhancers", People who reach out to enrich the lives of others, life enhancers lift others up, inspire and nurture others"
– Walt Disney, entrepreneur, animator, voice actor & film producer

"You must take personal responsibility. You cannot change the circumstances, the season or the wind, but you can change yourself"
– Jim Rohn, American entrepreneur, author, motivation speaker

No. 46

"Make excuses, give as little as possible, become tired, forsake the game plan and hurt others = DEFEAT"
– John C. Maxwell

"The winner's edge" is not in a gifted birth, a high IQ, or in talent, it is all in the attitude. Attitude is the criterion for success. When you change your attitude from doubt to confidence, "Everything" in your life will change for the better"
    – Denis Waitley, American motivational speaker, writer and consultant, author of "Seeds of Greatness" and "Winner's Edge"

"The only person responsible for the quality of life you are living is YOU!"
    – Jack Canfield, American author, motivational speaker, seminar leader, corporate trainer and entrepreneur

"Ninety-nine percent of all failures come from people who have a habit of making excuses"
– George Washington Carver, American botanist and inventor

No. 50

"Successful people face facts squarely. They do the uncomfortable and take steps to create their desired outcomes"
– Jack Canfield

"If you want to get from where you are to where you want to be, you're going to have to take a risk"
– Jack Canfield

No. 52

"The best gift you can give your family is to have your emotional, mental and spiritual health intact"
– Joyce Meyer

"You can't say you love Jesus and
then go out and live and act like the
devil. You can't say you're a Christian
and then keep on living a self-centered life'
– Rick Warren

No. 54

"The greatest gift you can give
someone is to be present, to "be"
with them, when you are "with"
them"
– Toni Wilkey (My Yoga Instructor)

"Don't let people disrespect you. My Mom says don't open the door to the devil. Surround yourself with positive people"
– Cuba Gooding, Jr., American actor

"Pay any price to be in the presence
of extraordinary people!"
– Mike Murdock, "Mike" Murdock is
an American Contemporary Christian
singer-songwriter, televangelist and
pastor of the Wisdom Center ministry,
based in Haltom City, Texas

No. 57

"Service to others is the rent you pay
for your room here on earth"
– Muhammad Ali, American Olympic
and professional boxer and activist.
He is widely regarded as one of the
most significant and celebrated
sports figures of the 20th century

Conclusion

"My Candid Quotes" was inspired by my being entangled in several traumatic experiences simultaneously and well, powerful things happen.

I started seeking and reading quotes to help me find the stamina to get through this grim chapter of my life and a means to cope with the pain I was in. At the time, I sought out numerous books to help me with my situation and all this reading forged "My Candid Quotes."

Pain serves a profound objective in our lives and it is a choice to not ignore that pain, but to "feel" it and seek what intent it holds to support purpose and meaning for our lives.

Shockingly, because I sat with my pain daily and chose to understand that pain, I have experienced an explosive awakening. Let's put it this way, recently, I heard a speaker say, "Less than 2% of people invest in their self development" that one statement validated me on multiple levels. If you are lucky enough to find a person who is in this 2%, get them in your rolodex! and go get some Velcro!

You too can make a choice to empower and equip yourself with the right resources, tools and people necessary to live the life you could live.

Stay conscious! Stay aware! Stay growing!
Believe in yourself and stay in faith!

---Bobbi Hall

Acknowledgements

Thank you! my beautiful mesmerizing yoga instructor Toni Wilkey, who brings it! and inspires me each and every class she teaches!

Thank You! Andrea Siracusa, for sharing your soul every week after Yoga class. Because of your concern to help me, the accumulation of pieces of scratch paper with information about spiritual teachers you have sought and found, continues to grow. I especially thank you for your weekly confirmations, "Bobbi, you are doing the work! You will find your light in the dark!"

Thank you! Lionnel Yamentou, to be willing to mentor me, hold me accountable and support my journey to succeed at my dreams!

Thank you! my treasured friend Barry Brown, who lends an unconditional ear at the drop of a dime day or night and encourages me constantly to "Feel what you Feel!"

Thank you! "Mir" (Miriam) Vargas, for catching my tears every week, months! and reminding me "God brings new mercies every day!" as I withstood 3 simultaneous traumas.

Thank you! Micheline, our long conversations, your red hearts in your text and your unconditional "Love" minister medicine to my broken heart! "Love you!"

Thank you! "Theo", you are a find! In my time of need your willingness to comply with my price for a highlight and haircut on short notice I am forever grateful! Sharing our stories with one another fuels my spirit and validates me, "I am not crazy!" Your texts cheerleading me and supportir my dreams serves as ammunition to succeed! Get ready my friend, every successful author and speaker needs a savvy makeup artist and hairstylist

And mostly,

Thank you! Marilyn Kaplan, facilitator of my grief group whose expertise in "Grief" has: educated, comforted, validated and supported me during as she states each week in group, "Empirical research shows, the loss of a great love is by far the hardest and worst emotional pain and suffering we will ever experience." Marilyn, imbedded in me forever is your weekly summary on how to get out of the black hole of grief and heal and get your life light lit is to, "Feel and Deal" with our pain; and committing to do so, will result in a pay off we never could imagine. Hearing you say, "Pain is the price we pay for emotional freedom!" fuels me every day now and inspired me to write this book.

Marilyn, there are not enough words to let you know how the work you do and share at grief class has changed my life!

About the Author

As a result of yet another job loss due to bullying in 2012, (and have since experienced another in 2015/16) and years of repetitive job losses due to layoffs, I made a choice to join Toastmasters to help myself. I always knew my communication skills needed help, well, an over-haul. Joining Toastmasters changed my life. I have not only learned how to communicate more effectively, but during that process of learning, I un-veiled hidden talents, gifts, strengths and competencies I never knew I had. One single choice to invest in my self-improvement has dramatically changed the direction of my life.

Still going, still growing, Bobbi has achieved a CC-Competent Communicator, ACB-Competent Communicator Bronze and a CL-Competent Leadership credential in Toastmasters and plans to earn many more.

Bobbi is a published author and has many more books to write. She is the owner of "My Granny's Cookies." On the horizon, Bobbi's plans include working closely with a speaking coach to achieve her dream of being a paid speaker; sharing her message with college graduates and parents, "Don't' ignore your inner voices, learn to make better choices; book smarts are one thing, life smarts are another!"

As a result of making better choices, her dream of sharing her message is drawing near.

Lastly, if you were to ask me, "Bobbi, what do you know for sure?" I would say, "What I know for sure is, if we do not seek, we will not find; and in and of itself is against the laws of the universe. It is impractical to make good, right, healthy choices if we do not seek, and the reward in doing so, is that God…….will always provide the right resources, tools and "people" we need and exactly……… at the right time!!!!!

Bobbi has performed stand-up comedy; she participates in comedy improv classes, she is an incessant reader, a word junkie and an avid Yoga practitioner.

Seattle, 2012 Bobbi and her beauitful Mom!

Connect with the Author

☐ LinkedIn:

https://www.linkedin.com/in/barbara-lee-hall-2a94102?trk=hp-identity-photo

☐ Facebook:

https://www.facebook.com/barbara.hall.9678

Bobbi can be reached at:

E-mail address: hallbobet@aol.com

www.bobbihall.com

Dear Readers,

Please drop me a line and let me know what you thought of "My Candid Quotes!" I would love to hear from you!

Praying for you!

Bobbi

www.ingramcontent.com/pod-product-compliance
Lightning Source LLC
Chambersburg PA
CBHW071215280526
45787CB00002B/695